SEX POSITIONS: OVER 100 TRULY EXPLOSIVE TIPS

THIS IS A CARLTON BOOK

Text, illustrations and design copyright © 2001
Carlton Books Limited

This edition published by Carlton Books Limited 2001
20 Mortimer Street, London W1T 3JW

A CIP catalogue record for this book is available from
the British Library.
ISBN 1 84222 266 X

Printed in Singapore

Editorial Manager: **Venetia Penfold**
Art Director: **Penny Stock**
Senior Art Editor: **Barbara Zuñiga**
Project Editor: **Zia Mattocks**
Editor: **Jane Donovan**
Design: **DW Design, London**
Production Manager: **Garry Lewis**
Illustrator: **Nicola Slater**

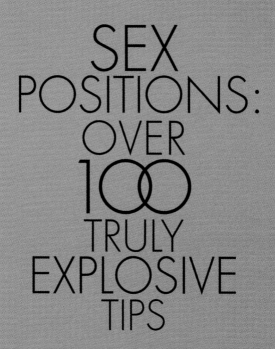

SEX POSITIONS: OVER 100 TRULY EXPLOSIVE TIPS

LISA SUSSMAN

CARLTON
BOOKS

RATINGS

To give you some guidelines, some of the following positions have been road tested and rated as follows:

Getting it Right

 Easy peasy.

★ ★ Read the directions carefully.

★ ★ ★ Sexpertise required.

Orgasmic Potential

 Sweet comfortable screw.

⇧ ⇧ A bit of a body rattler.

 A real sock roller.

1

Erotic Sex

In other words, enjoying happy horizontal hula simply for pleasure's sake.

SEX POSITION TIPS

Don't just settle for missionary monotony! Whether you're stuck in a sexual rut or just eager for some between-the-sheets experimentation, here's the ultimate guide to positioning yourself (and your partner) for the best sex ever. Let the games begin!

TAKE UP YOUR POSITIONS ...

For some **triple X-rated** twists on the old in and out.

MAN ON TOP (AKA 'MISSIONARY')

The Old Move: The classic man on top, woman beneath him, face-to-face position. He supports weight on his arms and you straddle his hips with your legs. It's great for easy thrusting (him) and creating close, intimate contact between you.

Make It Better: Do the knee–chest. Raise your legs so that your knees are pressed to your chest, then drape your legs over his shoulders. This will make your vagina longer, which will make his toes curl because he can penetrate you more deeply and give you more friction and pressure where you crave it most – on your vaginal lips and clitoris.

WOMAN ON TOP

The Old Move: This lets you stay in control and show your stuff. Simply sit on his penis and rotate those hips! Sitting is for sex in slow motion – the angles are all wrong for any sort of energetic thrusting. The man either sits in a chair or cross-legged on the floor, while you sit astride him, usually face to face, although it can work equally well if you face away from him. This position is good for caressing and intimacy.

Make It Better: Face his toes instead of his head. Then, as you lift yourself up and down, rotate your body in small circles. Tease him by using your vaginal lips to rub his erect penis – tantalize him by degrees until he's squirming.

3

STANDING

The Old Move: Standing is best for quickie trysts, but if he's much taller than you it's difficult to manage as he has to hold you up or you have to stand on a stool so his penis can reach your vagina.

Make It Better: Turn around and lean over to give him a delicious view of your derrière. Lift one leg sideways so he can slip inside you without having to twist, then close your legs slightly so he doesn't pop out. His hands can slip around to your clitoris to add a little extra heat.

SIDE BY SIDE (AKA 'SPOONING')

The Old Move: Side by side is a lovely cuddly move that's perfect for canoodling. The classic is spooning (lying on your side facing away from him so that he enters you from behind with his arms wrapped around you).

Make It Better: Have your lover lie on his back. Then, facing away from him, lower your crotch onto his (your arms should be stretched out behind you to support your weight). He encircles your waist with his legs and grips your thighs. Then you both roll over together onto your sides. He can then thrust gently into you …

REAR ENTRY (AKA 'DOGGIE')

The Old Move: The classic doggie-style position is a pleasure howler that gives ultra-deep penetration. You kneel on all fours and he slips in from behind …

Make It Better: Your partner lies on his back with a pillow beneath his head so he can watch all the action. Facing his feet, you straddle him. Then, placing your hands on the floor first, you back onto his penis. He holds your thighs or buttocks tightly while you thrust up and down the entire length of him. This is doing it doggie your way – you have maximum control while your partner gets to savour every sensation without working up too much sweat. It's a fantastic position for a truly intense G-spot orgasm.

PUSH YOUR BUTTONS ...

It still comes as a constant surprise to most guys, but intercourse isn't the best way for them to push you over the edge. Here's how to get him to trigger your orgasm switch.

HIT THE C NOTE

The clitoris is your hot button to bliss! Sex researcher Shere Hite found that over 75 per cent of women need to have this little bit of flesh stimulated in order to orgasm during sex.

- Doggie-style sex leaves his hands free to go walkies all over your breasts and clitoris (see tip 5).
- Twirling his penis around inside your vagina will slide it against your vaginal walls while his pubic bone grinds against your clitoris. You lie face up on the floor with a couple of pillows propping up your behind. Keep your knees half-bent, your legs splayed and your arms high above your head. Your partner enters you from a high angle, planting his hands on the floor beside your head. He moves around inside you in slow figure-of-eight motions.

- Putting your feet on his buttocks when you're in missionary mode will graze his pubic bone against your clitoris. Double your pleasure by raising your legs – the higher you lift them, the deeper the penetration against the front wall of your vagina, which is where your G-spot is.
- Spreading a little water-based KY Jelly on his penis, climbing on top of him (but without putting him inside you) and then moving back and forth will put enticing pressure on your clitoris.
- Lying on your back with your legs shut adds stimulation to your clitoris, and allows more friction with the nerve-rich surface of your vagina (not to mention his penis).
- To hit your clitoris every time – MEOW! – try the coital alignment technique (also known as the CAT). Instead of entering you straight on in the missionary position, he rides high so that his pubic bone – the hard surface just above the shaft of his penis – applies pressure to the rounded bit above your vagina (the hood) where the clitoris hides. Settling into a gentle mutual rhythm in which he rocks his pubic bone back and forth over your clitoris, rather than focusing so much on thrusting in and out, you get stimulated in all the right places.

G IS FOR GLORIOUS-ASM!

Researcher Beverly Whipple discovered that
halfway up the front wall of your vagina is
a soft swelling that will make you scream with
joy whenever it's pressed. These positions hit
the G-spot's bull's-eye every time:

- Sitting on top of him, facing his feet.
- Get on top and lean backwards and forwards.
- You lie on your stomach while he gently lies on
  top of you so he can penetrate you deeply from
  behind. You'll get G-
  spot and clitoral sparks
  at the same time!
- Get underneath him and
  have him place his hands beneath
  your hips and lift your whole pelvic
  area into the air.

GO TO YOUR AFE ZONE

The anterior fornix erogenous is located on the front wall of the vagina, a third of the way down from the cervix. Studies have found that 95 per cent of women had not only the most orgasms, but also the most intense ones of their lives when this area was caressed. Try these tips:

- Rear entry is the best move for hitting your Aaah … zone (see tip 5).
- Slipping a pillow underneath your hips when you're on the bottom tilts your pelvis forward and has the same effect.
- Lie on your back at the end of the bed and have him stand between your legs.
- Get into the missionary position (see tip 1) and hook your ankles around his shoulders or neck.
- When your AFE area is hit, this can result in waves of muscular contractions that seem hellbent on pushing your lover right out of you. When this happens, get him to push back. The more he pushes into you forcefully, the more intense your pleasure will be.

PENIS TICKLERS

These moves will make sure you give his favourite organ a total va-va-voom buzz during sex.

Whenever you're **on top of him**, facing his feet, consider this little trick: just as he's about to have his orgasm, grasp his toes and pull gently. It seems that the nerves in his toes are connected to the ones in his genitals so this extra stimulation increases the intensity of his ejaculation.

While on top (see tip 2), keep his penile skin **stretched tight** by holding it down at the base with your fingers. Imagine the heightened sensitivity you would experience if he stretched the skin around your exposed clitoris while thrusting against it with his pelvis and you'll understand why this manoeuvre can send him skyward!

When he's lying on top of you during sex, get him to **spread his legs** to take the pressure away from his testicles. If too compressed, they may become understimulated.

Lie flat on top of him with your legs in between his and squeeze your thighs tightly together. This way, you get to control how deeply he penetrates you while tantalizing the packed-with-nerve-endings head of his penis.

Double his pleasure by turning on his **G-spot**. When you're on top (see tip 2) or underneath (see tip 1), reach behind and press on the area between his backside and balls with your forefinger.

His penis is never happier than when it's **sliding inside** you as deeply as he possibly can. To give him the ground zero penetration, get into the missionary position (see tip 1) and lift your legs up and apart. The higher you can go, the further he'll be able to thrust – especially if you push into him with each stroke. (It helps if you wrap your legs around his shoulders.)

Sit up straight on top of him – you can face either way to do this. Now grind your pelvis around and around, back and forth. At the same time, squeeze your vaginal muscles tight until you vibrate him into sex heaven.

GET SYNCHRONIZED!

For a move even yummier than a five-star French meal, master the *soixante-neuf*.

16

Ask him to **hum** while he's giving you oral pleasure with his tongue on your pleasure knob.

17

Do the **60-minute** lick.
Ask for one slow, long, wet lick around your clitoris and return the favour on his love stick.

18

To prevent yourself from **gagging**
while pleasuring him, hold the base
of his penis as you suck. You'll control
how deeply his penis thrusts into your mouth.

Up his pleasure! Play with his nipples
or massage his buttocks.

19

BE A MOVIE STAR

Heat up the action in your bedroom by re-enacting these steamy love scenes.

NINE AND A HALF WEEKS

Fill your fridge with lots of sticky, squishy and yummy foods like strawberries, grapes, ice cream, chocolate mousse and orange juice. Take it in turns to blindfold each other and feed and drip the food over every orifice, alternating with tips 2, 5 AND 16–19).

OUT OF SIGHT

Substitute the car boot (trunk) for any cramped, dark space (a closet will do). Slip into a short, business-like dress, then jam your bodies together on the floor in a spoon position (see tip 4). He starts off by languidly stroking your thigh before roaming over the rest of your body.

THE POSTMAN ALWAYS RINGS TWICE

Sweep away everything from the kitchen table. Lie down on your back at the edge, extend your legs straight up, keeping them close together, and put your hands underneath your buttocks to elevate your pelvis. Standing up and gripping your legs for leverage and stability, your partner then enters you.

STRETCH IT OUT!

The looser and more supple your muscles, the more moves you can make. These stretches will help limber you into a sex gymnast!

POWER SQUATS

For overall improved **hip strength** and flexibility, stand with your feet slightly more than shoulder width apart and your arms straight out in front of you for balance. Bring your hips and backside back, bend your knees forward (no farther than your toes) and then straighten your legs. Do three sets of 15 repetitions a week.

BODY DIPS

Strengthen your triceps so that you can hold yourself up for longer periods when you're on top (see tip 2). Sit on a sturdy chair with its back securely against a wall. Hold the front of the seat on each side of your legs with the heels of your hands. Slide gently off the chair and pose, knees bent, with your elbows pointing towards the wall and your arms supporting your body. Lower your body, bending your elbows to a 90-degree angle and then push up. Do three sets of 15 repetitions a week.

HIP STRETCH

This exercise improves your **range of motion** when you're underneath (see tip 1). Lie on your back with your knees bent and your feet on the floor. Place your left foot comfortably across the middle of your right thigh, with your left thigh resting open. (For a better stretch, position your left foot closer to your hip.) Now pull your right thigh towards your chest for 20–30 seconds. Alternate sides for a total of three repetitions per side each week.

INNER THIGH AND HAMSTRING STRETCH

Limber yourself up for more athletic sexual positions. Sit **on the floor** with your legs pointing outwards in a 'V' position. For a wider stretch, place your hands behind you to support yourself and push your backside forwards, then lift it off the floor with small pelvic thrusts. Return to the start position, then turn your upper body towards one foot. Keeping your back as flat as possible, reach for that foot with your hands. Alternate sides for a total of three repetitions per side every week.

26

27

PC PUMPER

Strengthening your pubococcygeus (PC) muscles **enhances sexual pleasure**. Do this exercise regularly and you'll be able to milk his member to ecstasy while at the same time boosting your own orgasmic potential. Squeeze the muscles that control your urine flow for five seconds and then release. Do this for a minimum of 30 repetitions each day.

Sensual Sex

This is lovemaking that encompasses everything around you, so you slowly and steadily stimulate each other to intense peaks of sexual pleasure.

BEDROOM SEXESSORIES

Set the stage for your love ride ...

28

Before making love, place **mirrors** all around your room so you can see your reflections from all angles. Stand up (see tip 3) so you can press your body up against your reflection and get the erotic boost of seemingly making love to yourself.

29

Slip onto a luxurious **fur throw** or thick, soft rug to make love. The material feels very sensual to naked bodies.

All **fabrics** in the bedroom should be invitingly tactile – soft cotton, smooth silk, rich velvet, cool satin and knobbly bedspreads (for delicious friction).

Lightly **scent the room** or the sheets with a musky or flowery perfume. Everything else will smell fresh and clean. Eventually he'll begin to associate this scent with your lovemaking and you'll get him in the mood with just one whiff.

USE ALL YOUR SENSES

When you make love, indulge in a sensual feast.

Create the **sounds of seduction**. Have him get on top (see tip 1). Relax your vaginal muscles as he moves up and tighten them on the downswing. With practice, you'll make a loud, sexy, squishy sound. After orgasm, ask him to stretch out so he's lying flat on top of your body. The sound of his heartbeat will reverberate through your body.

Give the look of love. Sitting straight up on top of him gives you a sizzling full-eye view of each other.

Give off sexy scents. Slip into the missionary position (see tip 1) and lift your arms over your head to open your armpits (a sexy source of pheromones). One whiff will plunge you both into accelerated lust.

Indulge in a **tasty turn-on**. Lie on top of him so that your face is by his feet and your feet are by his head. Called a '20', this position lets you nibble each other's toes at the same time.

Discover the **power of touch**. Try making love in the dark. You have to feel your way, and not knowing where you'll be touched next can heighten the sexual tension. There's also something about being unable to see that makes your other senses respond more intensely to every sensation.

SLOW-HIM-DOWN SEX

Strike a pose and increase his staying power.

Change your position a few times during lovemaking. The momentary lapse can halt his momentum, which should curb early ejaculation.

Try the **Stop/Start Technique**. It doesn't matter what position you're in, but you should do most of the moving. With him lying as still as possible, gently move up and down until he nears his big moment. Stop if he's about to take an express trip to bliss until he's got himself in hand. But remember, thinking about something boring to delay ejaculation rarely works. Besides, it makes your love play slightly schizophrenic – you're turned on while he's obsessing about whether he can afford a new car! So, while all this stopping and starting is going on, he should be selfishly, happily and contentedly concentrating completely on his arousal. Once he can last as long as he wants to, he can start moving his hips as well.

38

Climbing on top and facing him (see tip 2) gives you total control over his – and your – sensations, especially if you ride your partner while kneeling or sitting. By keeping penetration shallow, you'll be able to set the pace as slow as you want without him jumping his orgasmic gun.

So long as he's at least **as tall as you**, you can have sex in a kneeling position, even if he isn't fully erect. He sits on the raised heels of his feet and you squat over him, face to face, with your thighs spread out. Now guide his penis inside you. Once he's in, you can take some of the weight off his back by leaning back on one arm while holding onto him with the other.

SLOW COMFORTABLE SCREWS

Well, you want this exquisite agony to go on for at least a few more hours, don't you?

To **slow things down** a bit, get on top (see tip 2) or underneath (see tip 1). Completely relax your vaginal muscles and place your legs flat alongside his. This makes for shallower thrusts, but keep your hips rocking so your bodies know you're still interested.

4²

Sit on your partner's lap with him inside you and distract each other. Lean out of the window and look at the garden, watch TV, talk about your day … The longer you can manage to ride it out, the better the end results.

Moving in **slow motion** makes you acutely aware of every part of the movement, from the muscles and body parts you're using to your weight shifts and your breathing – all of which you miss when you move too fast. Slip into a relaxing, sensual move such as the sidestroke, with both of you lying on your sides and him curled up behind you. Tell him to insert his penis slowly while you both focus on the feeling of your skin making contact, on your breathing and on the pleasurable pressure of his penis as it advances, little by little. Take a full minute to perform what you would usually do in just one or two seconds. You'll need to towel off after this one!

43

Get into **woman-on-top** mode (see tip 2), straddling his hips. Lower yourself onto his penis, but go no farther than the glans (the very tip of it). Then lift yourself back up in retreat and repeat nine times. On the tenth repetition, lower yourself all the way down onto his penis, letting him thrust fully into your vaginal canal. Pull yourself back up and begin your next set of attack and retreat, but this time allow eight shallow thrusts and two deep ones, followed by seven shallow and three deep thrusts, and so on. By the time you're taking ten deep thrusts from him, you'll have lost count. (If you don't have strong, steely thigh muscles, try leaning forward over your partner and use your abdominal muscles to lift your pelvis up and down until you collapse in delight.)

MOOD BUSTERS

Libido lift-offs, whatever your state of mind.

WHEN YOU'RE NEW LOVERS 45

For **first-time sex** – or first-time-together sex –
any position where he's on top (see tip 1) will
be the most comfortable and require the least
amount of effort from you (you have enough
to think about). Ease things along by placing
a pillow under your hips. Another tip you might
try is to push your pelvis down as he enters you
to help relax things down there.

WHEN YOU HAVE YOUR PERIOD

Assume **the spoon** (see tip 4). Then lift your
top leg while he shifts his lower body into a half-
kneeling position and enters you from behind.
This half-doggie, half-spooning hybrid combines
the cosy intimacy of lying side by side with G-spot-
rubbing rear entry without ever making an issue
of your period bloat.

46

47

WHEN YOU HAVE A HANGOVER

Getting the blood to rush straight to your head helps ease all that pounding, as will having a brain-melting orgasm. Studies show that an orgasm is the **best cure for a headache**. Start with your partner lying on his back. Facing his feet, straddle his hips on your knees and lower yourself onto his penis. Slowly extend your legs back towards his shoulders and relax your torso onto the bed or ground between his feet. Both sets of legs should now form an 'X' shape. Use your PC muscles (see tip 27) and move your buttocks up and down or back and forth to maintain his erection.

★ ★

**WHEN YOU'VE HAD AN ACNE
ATTACK OR EATEN GARLIC FOR LUNCH**
Head over heels is a sexy position that's not
face to face. Kneel down, cross your arms in
front of you and lean forward so that your
forearms rest on the ground and your derrière is in
the air (cushion your arms on a pillow if you wish).
Then rest your head on your arms. Your partner
stands behind you and lifts your legs up by your
knees until you're almost completely vertical,
then he enters you from behind.

49

WHEN YOU HAVE PREMENSTRUAL SYNDROME

Studies have discovered two things: (1) boosted hormone levels means that right before your period is a high-octane time for you to make whoopee; and (2) an orgasm is a great cure for cramp. So, assume the position. Ask your lover to lie on his back on the bed and slowly squat onto his erect penis, facing his feet. Lean back as far as you can, being careful not to strain your lower back, and snuggle up against his chest. Reach back with your hands and caress his head. Your (bloated) tummy will look amazingly thin.

WHEN YOU'RE FEELING FAT

Try a classic pose to make you look (and feel) sexy and **voluptuous**. Make love in a side-to-side position, propped up on your elbow with the knee of your top leg resting on the bed. To your lover, your waist will look tiny and your hips will seem ultra-curvy.

WHEN YOU'RE IN A SINGLE BED

Start in the **missionary position** (see tip 1) and, with your legs and arms wrapped around him, gently roll over to one side. If there's too much weight on your bottom leg, you can carefully slip your legs between his.

3

Intimate Sex

Even the most vertically-challenged relationship can get stuck in the middle of orgasmic nowhere after a while. Not to worry. All you need to get your return ticket to Ecstasy-ville are a few smooth moves. Slip any of the following into your next lovefest and let the pleasure ride begin!

SPICE IT UP

To get things sizzling again, here are some new positions for old lovers that are guaranteed to get the sparks flying.

THE TWISTER

Your partner lies on his back with his legs spread slightly and his head propped up with a pillow. Start by lying on your back next to him, then swing your legs over his body crosswise and keep them close together so your legs are positioned perpendicular to his. Sit on his lap and lean back on your arms for support. Open your legs slightly as he enters you and begin making slow, swivelling, **corkscrew motions**.

THE LEG LIFT

Your guy sits on the floor, his palms on the ground behind him and his fingers pointing away from him. His legs are splayed open and his knees are slightly bent. Placing your hands on the floor for support, you face him and straddle his lap. Raise your legs so your right leg rests on his left shoulder and your left leg is on his right shoulder. Keep your bodies close together so he doesn't slip out. The angle of his dangle will bring on deep **G-spot orgasms**.

★ ★ ★

54

THE BONDER

You and your guy lie on your sides, facing each other. Now lean in and **scissor** your legs together. While thrusting, hold on close to each other for leverage and to create super-close friction. Rather than typical in-and-out thrusting, this sexual scissoring lets you and your guy please each other with grinding, circular motions.

55 Aim to try out **ten new positions** a month (check out the rest of this book for ideas).

BODY BOOGIE

Physically, not all lovers are perfect matches. Here's how to mesh your bodies in the throes of love.

WHEN YOU'RE TALLER THAN HIM

He sits on the floor with his arms stretched out behind him for support and his legs crossed loosely. You climb onto his lap so you're straddling him in a kneeling position. Hold onto his shoulders as you lower yourself onto his erect penis, Keep your bodies extremely close together as **you take control** of the timing and speed of the thrusting.

WHEN HE'S A LOT TALLER THAN YOU

Sitting on top of him (see tip 2) ensures your love organs **stay connected**.

58

**WHEN HE HAS A LAGER GUT
OR YOU'RE HEAVIER THAN HIM**

A side move will let you work around your
bulges. Lie on your back with your man to
your right. He lies on his left-hand side. Bend
and lift your right leg up. Your man arranges
his right leg over your left and inserting his penis
in this position allows a nice leisurely pace. Crank
up the pleasure factor by grinding your buttocks
tantalizingly **against his pelvis**.

WHEN HE PACKS A BIG ONE!

If your man has a **large penis**, lying flat on top of him with your legs in between his and squeezing your thighs tightly together lets you control how deeply he penetrates you, while making sure his penis still gets fully massaged.

WHEN HIS PENIS IS PUNY

The **size** of a penis has very little to do with satisfying a woman. All it takes is 4–5 centimetres (1^1/$_2$–2 inches) to reach the super-sensitive nerve endings in your vagina. And nearly every penis, no mater how tiny when flaccid, is between 12.5 and 17.5 centimetres (5 and 7 inches) when erect. But you can still make it easier for him – and for you – by opting for a rear-entry position (see tip 5), which will make the most of what he has. Being on top (see tip 2) will also 'shorten' your vagina.

60

PUTTING IN THE PACES

According to studies, it's not the size of his package that counts – it's what you both do with it once it's in you that's the real key to how loud you'll be screaming with joy …

Allow him to penetrate you **more deeply**. Place pillows under your hips so your entire body is on an incline with your crotch angled up in the air.

When you're underneath, **clench your buttocks**. You'll lift your pelvis a little way off the bed and increase the blood flow to your pelvic area, making orgasm easier.

More thrusting does not necessarily mean more fun! Instead, get your man to rock your world by **rocking back and forth**.

The most **sensitive nerve endings** are near the opening of the vagina and in the head of the penis. So bring on a Big O by keeping penetration shallow.

65

After you've come and your vagina has **tightened** but your contractions are still going, ask him to keep on stroking inside your vagina until they stop. He should then quickly move to your clitoris and massage it. On the point of no return, ask him to put his fingers inside you again. Get ready to dissolve with pleasure!

To give him a rest while keeping him hot, ask him to **stop** while you do all the thrusting.

66

ORGASMS IN 0 to SEXTY

Here are some hurrying-up helpers for when you're having sex against the clock!

Do it in the morning! You're already horizontal, you have less clothes on to worry about, his testosterone level is highest, and you'll be in a carefree, glowing mood for the rest of the day.

67

68

Dress for speed: wear easy-to-unzip trousers (him) and a skirt with no underwear and definitely no tights (you).

When giving each other some simultaneous mouth sex, **keep pace together** by putting on some music with a strong, steady beat (pretty much anything from the 1970s will do).

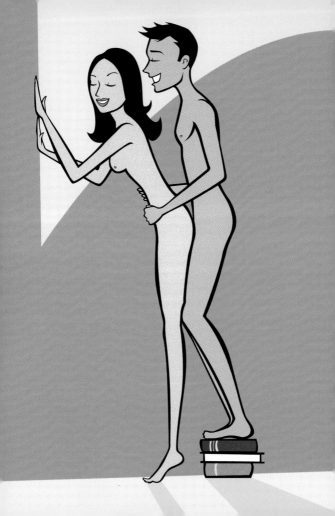

Rear entry is best from a standing position if space is tight, but it can be tricky to match up your love organs if you and your man are different heights. For guaranteed satisfaction, face away from him and bend over so that your hands are flat on the floor and your weight is forward (or just lean against a wall).

70

4

Daring Sex

Push your acts of amour to the utmost limit. Buckle up and get ready for an action-packed ride! Here, anything goes … but proceed at your own risk – you could find yourself in a whole new position, like court!

MARATHON MOMENTS

Try some of the following moves to make your carnal connection last from here to eternity …

Use a water-based **lubricant** like KY Jelly to increase the length of time you're able to have sex without risk of soreness.

Leaning away from each other is the perfect beginning for a **lovemaking epic**, although it probably won't give either of you a pulse-pumping orgasm. Start off by sitting on top of your man, facing him. Both of you then fall back in opposite directions supporting your weight on your elbows or hands, or you can lie flat on your back (whatever makes you happy). He gently thrusts from below for as long as your hearts desire (or his penis holds out), whichever comes first!

★ ★

Do the chain. Lie back with
your legs up, open and wide apart
while your lover lowers himself on you face
down, with his head by your feet and his legs
over your hips so that his feet are on either side of
your shoulders. You can rest your legs on his back
and play with his balls as he thrusts backwards. For a
real joygasmic thrill, hold on to his hips and pull
yourself up in the middle of your love play to give
your insides – and his penis – a total massage.

STAY IN CONTROL

Daring sex doesn't mean taking stupid risks. Make your contraception work for you and enjoy the double thrill of being sassy and sexy.

BE SAFE

The best position for sex is a safe one. Condoms are your best protection from AIDS, chlamydia and most other sexually transmitted diseases (STDs).

THE PILL

By suppressing ovulation, the Pill can lower your levels of testosterone. As a result, some women may feel a dip in desire. Any rear entry position (see tip 5) gives him access to play with your clitoris as he thrusts to re-rev your cravings.

INTRAUTERINE DEVICE (IUD)

The IUD can sometimes make sex a bit dry, which can be uncomfortable. Keep things sweet and sexy by using a side-entry position where your legs are interlocked. (He has one leg on the bottom, your lower leg comes next, then his top leg, then yours). Get him to grab your backside and hold you close to keep things tight and tantalizing.

DIAPHRAGM

Depending on the fit, this barrier device may hinder access to the area that requires stimulation. Sitting on top and leaning back so that your ankles rest on his shoulders will fully open your vagina and make sure his penis doesn't miss this hot spot during intercourse.

CERVICAL CAP

This device gives him free access to your vagina, so make good use of it! Have him come at you from behind, then rotate your hips in small, circular movements to ensure his penis bumps every part of your vaginal canal.

MALE CONDOM

Some men report reduced sensations from condoms, so really up his pleasure by sitting on top of him and leaning back and forth during sex to literally massage his penis with your vagina.

FEMALE CONDOM

Some women find that the ring on the base of the female condom stimulates their clitoris during sex. Make sure of this by using a man-on-top position with him riding slightly high on you (see tip 6/the CAT).

GET OUT OF BED!

Incredibly erotic hot spots for love trysts around the house will make you leap out of bed.

SOFA STRADDLER

Your partner **sits back on a sofa** (or comfy chair) as you straddle his lap with your legs splayed apart and your knees bent up against his chest. Then lean back so that you're almost upside-down, with your arms stretched behind you all the way to the floor to support your weight. Thrust back and forth, opening and closing your legs and clamping your PC muscles (see tip 27) around him. When you're ready for him to hit his passion peak, send him soaring by squeezing your PC muscles when he's completely inside you.

81

STAIR STOPPER

Kneel in front of your partner on the landing
of a staircase, with both of you facing the stairs.
While you reach up and hold onto each side of the
staircase for support (or to the stairs themselves),
he holds your hips and penetrates you from behind.
Be careful not to pull the banisters away!

82

TABLE ROCKER

You **sit on a dresser** or table and he stands,
facing you. Now edge yourself down until he
can comfortably slip inside you. This body-rocking
move angles your vagina just right for a two-for-one
G-spot/clit climax.

84

WATER PLAY

He gets in the **bath** first with his back to one end, his legs spread out in front of him and his knees slightly bent. (If your bath has taps at one end, make sure this is the way his back is facing.) Now you get in, sitting so you're facing him, with your arms propping you up from behind. Position your legs so they're bent on either side of him and your feet are resting lightly against the edge of the bath (if the bath isn't big enough to get a stable surface, just wrap your legs around his waist). Push your pelvis forward, lift your hips a little and use one hand to put him inside you.

85

ON THE WASHING MACHINE

Have him sit on the washing machine. Then climb onto his lap, facing away from him (he can keep you in place by encircling you in his arms). Flip on the **spin cycle** and get ready to vibrate yourselves to a deliciously dirty climax.

THE GREAT OUTDOORS

Whatever the scenery, the lack of a ceiling (and the risk of being spotted) will intensify the experience outside.

If you're going to have **sex outdoors** in any position other than standing, bring a soft blanket with you. Avoid using bug spray and sun block until afterwards – both taste awful!

ON THE BEACH

Making love on the beach can be a truly sexy. Use the **rhythm of the waves** to roll from underneath to on top and back again – you'll come oceans!

ON A PARK BENCH

Wear a long, floaty skirt **without underwear** and have him wear easy-access shorts. Keep things discreet by lifting your skirt, sitting on his lap side-saddle and wriggling gently until you achieve the desired effect.

ON THE GRASS

Relax on your stomach and elbows, and get your man to lie on top of you with his weight on his arms. Raise your hips slightly to increase penetration (and avoid ants in your pants!).

ON A CAR BONNET

Make sure the engine is cool and the car alarm is switched off! Then lie back with your hips at the edge of **the bonnet** and your legs spread wide. He stands between your legs, lifts them and penetrates you. Pull up to the bumper, baby!

IN A PARK

Stand facing a wall or tree with your feet about 45 centimetres (18 inches) apart. He stands behind you, bends his knees (unless you're taller than him) and enters you from below. If he wants to **show off**, he can hold your hips to steady himself and lean back, while you lean forward against the wall.

IN AN ALLEYWAY, FITTING ROOM OR OTHER NON-LIE-DOWN ZONE

He squats on his heels and **you sit**, facing him, on his upper thighs with your weight on your feet. Wrap your arms around him for balance. You'd better make this one a quickie!

92

GO WILD

Rev up the raunch with some lurve tools and keep things sweet between the sheets.

There's nothing like **feathers to tickle** his fancy. Have a wide assortment handy – a feather duster, a boa, a quill, a peacock feather. Lightly brush over his whole love organ area while you sit on top of him (see tip 2). To really make him squirm with delight, concentrate on the spot where his penis meets his balls.

raising orgasm. Or try something bubbly like soda or champagne. **Give him a lap dance**. Dress in crotchless panties and have your partner lean back on a strong, comfortable chair. Facing him and with your hands behind you resting on his knees, snuggle onto his lap. Lift your ankles up to rest on his shoulders. Start gyrating by inching yourself back and forth against his erect member. Slip him in and out of you to drive him wild with desire.

94

Put a small scoop of your favourite **ice scream** in your vagina, lie back and slip him inside you. Alternate with dripping warm – but not hot – wax over your bodies (be very careful, you don't want to cause third-degree burns!) to make your blood vessels dance with delight and give him a temperature-raising orgasm. Or try something bubbly like soda or champagne.

95

Have him **tie** your hands and feet together, then set you up on your elbows and knees. He then comes from behind to ravish you mercilessly while you love every minute of it.

96 **97**

If you have **long hair**, climb on top of him (see tip 2) so you can seductively brush it back and forth across his body during sex.

Get fruity! A mashed banana or peaches inserted in your vagina is a delightful invitation for him to whoosh his penis around in it. Once you climax, switch to the 69 position for sweet afters.

Cool down your vagina with a **frozen-yoghurt** or flavoured-ice stick, then replace it with his penis. The heat of his organ against your icy skin will make it a sizzling sensation.

Wrap a **silk scarf** around your hand to stroke him. Rub it all over his body, tying it around his penis or testicles. Then use it to tie his hands or feet together and climb on top of him (see tip 2).

Get on the fast track to ecstasy! Lie back in the missionary position (see tip 1) and have him slip a **vibrator** against the base of your clitoris while he's inside you. He'll be able to feel the vibrations too and soon you'll both be pulsating with pleasure.

JOIN THE CLUB

To become a member, the only requirement is body-blistering sex!

THE MILE-UNDER CLUB

Go scuba diving in warm water so you can wear just a bathing suit (this move also works well in waist-high water). Push the crotch of your bathing suit aside, then wrap your legs tightly around his waist (the water will make you lighter than air). Go with the flow, using the motion of the water to rock you up and down.

102

103

THE MILE-HIGH CLUB

Do it **on a plane** by sneaking off to the bathroom. Stand with your back to him and lean over the sink so he can swoop in from behind. Bonus: you can watch yourself in the mirror – this beats flying first class every time!

104

THE FAST-LANE CLUB

If you **get the hots** while driving your car, pull over in a secluded spot and jump on his lap. You can either face him with your knees pushed against your chest and your feet on the seat or hooked over the neck rest, or face away from him with your feet on the car floor. Either way, you won't be able to get much movement, so squeeze your thighs to increase the pressure on your love organs.

105

THE FAR-OUT CLUB

Doing it **in a boat** is like making love on a waterbed! But the position you choose isn't as important as how you position yourselves in the boat. Stand close to the centre of the boat and keep your body low. Motor boats and catamarans are the most stable, canoes the least. (Whatever you do, don't remove personal flotation devices and make sure you can both swim!)

5

Spiritual Sex

Your guide to nookie nirvana. Get ready to have the best, most satisfying, intense, mind-blowing sexual experience of your life. But be warned – there's no such thing as a spiritual quickie. Love made Eastern-style can last for hours (read: hours of pure soul-in-sync bliss … mmmm!).

SAY OHM-MY-GOD!

Prime your body for divine passion.

THE BRIDGE

Sit face to face with your legs wrapped around each other's backs. Slip him inside you and snuggle in by grasping each other's elbows, then lean back. Now see if you can tilt your head far enough back to rest it on the floor. Try to remain still and concentrate on your bodies, completely connecting the sexual energies flowing through you.

106

THE JUMPING FROG

Start in the standard missionary position (see tip 1). He then rises up on **all fours**, and you raise your pelvis to meet his penis. As he stays stationary, start moving your hips up and down to get him jumping.

107

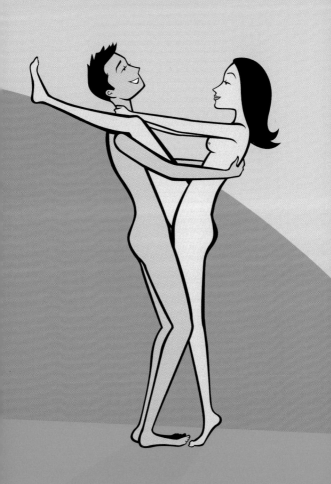

THE CRANE

Stand **facing your partner** with your left foot
turned out, perpendicular to your sweetheart,
and your right foot forward. His legs should be
slightly bent, spaced about 1 metre (3 feet) apart.
With your arms resting on his shoulders and his
arms around your lower back, slowly pull your
right leg up and prop your right foot on his
shoulder. Once he penetrates you, ease into
the vertical split by sliding your right calf as
far up his shoulder as you comfortably can.

THE THREE-POINTED STAR

Lie **on your back** with your left leg
extended straight up in the air and your
right leg stretched out to your right on
the floor, perpendicular to your body. Reach
out across the floor with your right hand and
clasp your right knee, forming a triangle with
your right side, right leg and right arm. Your
partner crouches at the bottom and enters you.

READ YOUR HOROSCOPE

Follow your zodiac to discover the most out-of-this-world position for you …

ARIES

An ultra-physical lover who like to take charge of her own sexuality.

Best Move: Anything on top (see tip 2) that lets you masturbate yourself to orgasm while controlling the thrusting.

TAURUS

A sensual lover who likes sex to last.

Best Move: A side-by-side position (see tip 4) that lets you do it just how you like it: in long, lazy bouts, with plenty of time out for kissing and caressing.

GEMINI

She likes variety, and lots of it!

Best Move: Start on top, so you're sitting straight up facing your lover. You can then lean forwards and backwards, or even swivel around to face his feet or roll over so you're underneath.

CANCER

A shy lover – she's never the aggressor.

Best Move: The classic missionary position (see tip 1) lets you feel like you're being seduced, especially if he holds your hands tight above your head.

LEO

She loves the foreplay almost even more than she enjoys the intercourse.

Best Move: Doing the 69 really lets you indulge your oral side.

VIRGO

Sexually mercurial, the Virgo lover likes to try many different things.
Best Move: Just about anything will spark your interest – and orgasms!

LIBRA

For her, it's all about the pursuit of pleasure …
Best Move: Rear entry (see tip 5), so you or your lover can caress your clitoris at the same time.

SCORPIO

Lusty and passionate, she likes to direct the action.
Best Move: Anything that puts you on top and in control of the depth and pace.

SAGITTARIUS

A strong lover, she enjoys strenuous intercourse and will make love through the night.

Best Move: Sitting on top and leaning back so you can see your lover as he massages your clitoris and breasts.

CAPRICORN

A straightforward and direct lover, she doesn't relish complicated sex.

Best move: The straightforward man-on-top move keeps things simple and sexy for you.

AQUARIUS

Curious and uninhibited, she likes to make love whenever – and wherever – the urge strikes.

Best Move: Usually standing and leaning over for a sexy quickie.

PISCES

An unusually creative lover who believes in the possibility of total ecstasy.

Best Move: You take classic poses just that little bit further. Lifting your legs over his shoulders while sitting on top of him, or sitting on his lap with your legs intertwined are two ways you might put your own stamp on making love (see tips 1–5 for more ideas).